BRAINSTORM

from STROKE to my TRUSTING place

BRAINSTORM

from STROKE to my TRUSTING place

Joanne M. Susi

S.I.T.E.

PUBLISHING

Brainstorm: From STROKE to my TRUSTING place
Author: Joanne M. Susi
Email: coachjsusi@gmail.com

First Trade Edition - Published 2015
Printed in the United States and United Kingdom by
Lightning Source

Published by:
SITE Publishing
7330 Staples Mill Road (PMB/#212)
Richmond, VA, 23228-4110
www.sitepublishingtoday.com
sitepublishingtoday@gmail.com

Cover/Interior Design: SITE Publishing

ISBN-13 - 978-0-9796241-5-5
ISBN-10 - 0979624150
Library of Congress Control Number: 2015935570

Dedication

This book is dedicated to my three grown children whom I call my magical three, Christopher, Shelly and Brian, thank you for all your support through the years especially during and after the stroke. You have been my reason for living these past 41 years since the birth of my first, Christopher. Everything I do, I do with your best interest at heart. Plus I was not ready to leave you guys six years ago, I don't think I will ever be ready; I love you more than words can say. I pray the day will come when you see in yourselves what I have seen since your birth; pure love, joy, fun, compassion, understanding and full out passion for life. You never cease to take my breath away with your divine powers and earthly antics or as you like to say shenanigans! You are blessed more than you can see.

I also dedicate this book to my amazing grandson Darren and YOU, the reader for you have provided me the inspiration and purpose to write this book; may you be inspired and courageous enough to live the life of your dreams!

Introduction

Every one of us has a story. I have just decided to write mine with the desire and intention of sharing my story to hopefully inspire at least one of you. Or at least help you understand and be comforted with your story and world. None of us are perfect human beings, but our souls are perfect and carry all the wisdom we need in life, we just don't know that because we were not taught it. God bless our parents and those in authority over us during our growing-up years, they did the best they could; as do we with where we are on our evolutionary journey in life. I hope that in reading this book you will see my journey and how my stroke has helped me evolve into a better person with a deeper faith, understanding and knowingness of life. I am no better or different than you, who is reading this now.

Life can be difficult especially when we are unaware of how it all works and that we are spiritual beings having a human experience. And as humans we all have our coping methods healthy and unhealthy as well as legal and illegal to get through the difficult times. During my whole life I have used a few coping mechanisms, thank God they are legal but not always healthy or good for me.

I used food as one of my coping tools during my three year stay in the nursing home following my stroke and that is my story. I must admit in all fairness to you and myself, I struggle every day to stay out of frustration. I am constantly working through facing my weaknesses — physical, spiritual and emotional. And my biggest seems to be keeping my papers organized, difficult before the stroke now it seems more so with not having full use of my left hand and arm as I am writing this book. However, I believe that is just an excuse that I will overcome. I pray you also will decide to overcome your excuses and step into your beautiful powerful divine self. As Dr. Wayne Dyer says, "Excuses Begone!"

So what and where is the Trusting Place? It is the place in our heart and soul that is connected with God. It is where our faith takes over our ego. It is the place of extreme peace. It is our heaven on earth. It is where we carry all our wisdom; it is our worry-free space. I had been searching for it almost my whole life and finally found it after my stroke. This is one big reason to be grateful for my stroke although I have myriad reasons for my gratitude. As you read through this book, I hope you will see my reasons and how my perspective works to keep me thriving to this very moment six years later.

And it all started...

Chapter 1
The Day Before Easter

'Twas the day before Easter, March 22, 2008, I wasn't feeling great. I was sitting on the couch wondering if I should go to the store as usual when the voice inside my head said, "Just go to Whole Foods as you always do on Saturdays!" So I put my jacket on, got in my car and off I went to Whole Foods. I was quite excited about buying salmon and vegetables to roast for dinner so I went thru the produce aisle to pick out the veggies I wanted to roast, then picked out a piece of salmon to grill. Continuing through the store, I arrived at the bakery counter, leaning over to pick out a muffin from the case. All of a sudden, my eyes went blurry; I kept blinking hoping it was my contact lenses that needed some moisture. Then that same voice told me to just go to the cash register to check out and go home.

While I was standing in line my cell phone rang; trying to get it out of my purse was difficult as my legs were shaking. The woman who was bagging groceries came up behind me, put her arms around my waist and said in my ear, "Don't worry, I won't let you fall." She then got a chair for me to sit in while someone called an ambulance. I was flooded with emotions as she put her arms around my waist and spoke those words of comfort to me. I was scared, but felt assured I was okay. I was also very embarrassed that this was happening to me and perhaps a bit angry. To this day I have not had the chance to thank this kind, thoughtful earth angel of a woman. My friend, Kinsey, was in the store one day, wearing the bracelet made for my fundraiser and a woman at the register noticed it on her wrist and told her she liked it and asked where she got it. When Kinsey explained where it came from, the woman excitedly explained she was the woman who had helped me that day I had the stroke in Whole Foods. So they talked a bit and she told Kinsey her name is Anne and had been wondering about me. I loved hearing the story from Kinsey about their meeting each other and Kinsey in all her generosity, gave her bracelet to Anne.

The EMT'S came quickly, put me in the ambulance and off we went to Milford Hospital, the closest hospital to that Whole Foods. As I was driving to the hospital to show you how my mind works, this is what I thought; I will get to the hospital, they will check me out to find everything okay and take me back to Whole Foods so I could buy my groceries, go home and cook the delicious dinner I had planned for myself. Being a single woman, I made sure to have a date with myself every Saturday night, by making a nice meal and perhaps watching a chick flick or something spiritual since my spirituality was and is of most importance to me.

Before I knew it my oldest son, Christopher was in the ER with me while the doctor was telling me I had a stroke and he thought I should have a shot of TPA, a clot busting drug. My son, who is scared of medicine immediately said, "Mom you don't need that; you can fix this yourself!" The doctor of course said I could not and I told both I wanted the shot. God bless Christopher's belief in me! Or perhaps misunderstanding of me! After the shot, my left arm and leg worked better. At first they were limp, no pain thank goodness, but not much movement. Soon after the doctor told me I would be air-lifted to Mass General Hospital where he felt I would receive the best care. The helicopter ride was very interesting even though I was a bit scared; they put earplugs in my ears to drown out the loud sound of the helicopter.

The next thing I remember is waking up in a room in ICU looking up seeing my sister and two brothers looking down at me as well as two friends who told the hospital they were siblings of mine—the only way to get into ICU. I was astonished but pleased to see them all. To this day I am not sure they fully understand the impact of comfort they brought me by being there. A thought just crossed my mind; we pay our respects at wakes and funerals to the dead, why is it we don't understand the importance of spending time with loved ones while they are here and alive, this is time well spent for it touches everyone's hearts. I also remember appreciating the nurses caring for me in the ICU. They were warm, caring and competent from my perspective. I was soon moved to the neurology floor.

My daughter was living and working in New Hampshire. Bless her heart, she immediately quit her job and moved back to MA as soon as she heard about my situation. She made sure to be in that hospital with me every day. Watching over me and making sure I was well cared for. Boy does she have a story to tell about her experiences with hospital staff! I am hoping she writes her story as I am writing mine. After a few days, (I think. I haven't much concept of time during those days following the first stroke) I was not feeling very well, a bit of a headache and did vomit once. My daughter knew something was very wrong when she came into my room and took one look at me, she told the nurses and they said I was just a bit off but was okay. Shelly would not leave my side. She tells me my eyes started to roll and then I was gone; the doctors had to revive me. It was then they realized I had a hemorrhagic stroke. A side note here; I do not have a conscious memory of a NDE (Near Death Experience) But I do have a knowingness that I spoke with God. I believe I was given a choice of what I wanted; to remain dead or go back to my body on earth. So as you can see my choice was to come back, I had unfinished business, more to experience and teach. This is the reason to share my story.

So while I believe I was conversing with God, the doctors and my children were in the conference room of the hospital trying to decide what to do about the bleeding in my brain. The doctors presented all scenarios to the kids. Shelly tells me that after a while she turned to one of the neurosurgeons and asked, "If this were your mother what would you do?" He immediately responded, "She would be on the operating table right now. With that Shelly said, "Then get up now, there is no time to waste and get my mother in that operating room right now!" I love Shelly; she is a bulldog when it comes to protecting her loved ones! Everyone needs an advocate like my beautiful daughter!

So off they took me to the OR to perform brain surgery to stop the bleeding in my brain. Eight hours later when surgery was over the doctors told my children all was well but they thought I might never walk again. With that again Shelly piped right up saying to the neurosurgeon, "Oh you don't know my mother!" I remember waking up and seeing my good friend Kinsey there waiting for me to wake. I remember telling her, "I am going to be better than before; better spiritually, physically, emotionally and mentally." How did I know that? I think it was my conversation with God that assured me of what I believed.

Chapter 2
Off To Spaulding Rehab Hospital

After the operation I was sent to Spaulding Rehab Hospital for more recuperating along with physical, occupational, and speech therapy. I had to learn how to walk again, along with learning how to get up out of and into bed. One of the most important things I have learned is the power of focus. I had to focus when walking to avoid falling.

To this day, I still must focus when doing anything. As sad as it might be we truly cannot multi-task and do it well. In order to do anything correctly, we must focus on that one thing. This is how we create accidents or make mistakes without even realizing; our brains cannot focus on more than one thing at a time. I digress a bit from the chronological occurrences following my stroke.

Spaulding provided amazing help and support from day one. All staff is well trained to care for patients with limitations, knowing how to help them transfer. For example, at first I needed help getting out of bed and into a wheelchair, very scary at first. I thought I would not ever be able to do it by myself, but they taught me how. I had a full daily schedule of physical, occupational, and speech therapy. I loved the structure and discipline of it all. Although quite often I was so tired, I did not want to do my therapy. I had to push myself many days. How I did that was with my thinking; I knew I wanted to get better and I knew I had to do my part in allowing that to happen. So the lesson here is it takes clarity on what you want then commitment and discipline to carry out the action steps to reach a goal. It helped make me feel I was doing my part in getting better. I was and still am a disciplined, structured woman who loves to exercise.

Chapter 3
Discovery of Atrial Fibulation

One day when working with my physical therapist, I noticed my heart beating a bit faster than normal. I thought it was because I was exercising, but my daughter took one look at me and immediately made me sit down and went to get the doctor. My heart was racing and the cardiologist was quickly called to help. They were working on me for some time to get my heart beat back to normal. I remember Shelly frantically watching to make sure I was ok. I kept telling her not to worry, I was okay. I knew I was not going to die, but I could see on her face she was not so sure. Soon I was put on an ambulance with paramedics to take me back to Mass General Hospital. After a few days of observation, it was decided I needed a pacemaker and medication to control my Atrial Fibulation. After that installation, I was sent back to Spaulding Rehab to continue my rehabilitation. I was extremely well cared for at Spaulding. It is no kidding when you hear they are the best! I have done outpatient Physical and Occupational therapy in the Braintree, MA location. I could not ask for a better service. They are experts in Neuro patients and most importantly believe what I believe—that I will be back 100%. Now I must let you know, insurance puts a limit on how many visits one can have with therapy, this can put a halt to the recuperation after a stroke or any brain injury. What is most important after the incidence is continued support to help with keeping one's spirits up and to not give up. Again it is not just about the physical progress which is how the insurance companies decide on payments for therapies. Again, we all need a holistic approach for well-being; mind, body and SOUL all need to be fed and cared for!

Spaulding cared for me until I no longer needed acute hospital care and was then recommended to go to a skilled nursing facility where I could receive Physical and Occupational therapy. So out Shelly went all by herself to find the best nursing facility for me to go to. She decided on Highgate Manor Nursing Home in Dedham, MA.

I remember the day I left Spaulding was a very sad and difficult day for me. It was like my security blanket was being taken away from me. I now understand how a baby must feel when their bottle, binky, blanket or anything they are attached to is taken away. When your feeling of security is gone, it is most scary. But as usual, I sucked it up and knew all would be fine as it always is. I was alive for God's sake! What is there to complain about? I am not a baby; I am a grown woman who has cared for herself her whole life, surviving breast cancer twice leading to a double mastectomy as well as two divorces, supporting myself, and starting my own coaching practice. I know I have courage and can do anything I set my mind to, so there was no room to be scared, it was just another change.

And as I have taught many people, the one thing you

can count on in life is change. So we best be prepared in order to survive. Now there are many things that helped me survive, even to this day: First is my constant faith and belief in God, as well as belief in myself; my determination and stubbornness; my mindset, which makes me believe I can do anything I want to do; my glass-half-full attitude; the unwavering love of my three grown children (who I call my Magical Three); and my spiritual books, especially all of **Neal Donald Walsch's Conversations With God** books.

Also what is most important to me is to feed myself daily with only positive things, like inspirational newsletters and quotes plus not watch the news filled with negativity. For television, I will only watch shows that are uplifting with their entertainment, comedies, **Dancing with the Stars, The Voice, PBS**, etc.

Chapter 4
I Ate My Way Through The
Nursing Home

I spent three years in Highgate Manor waiting for an appropriate apartment to live in independently. I must admit, living in a nursing home is not the worst thing in the world, but it is not the best place either.

Now I would like you to hear what it is like to live in a nursing home: There is a feeling you are not important and actually sometimes a pain to very busy overworked staff. I felt vulnerable and scared many times. Not being able to get around on my own sucked. If I had to go to the bathroom, I needed a staff to help me transfer from my bed to my wheelchair, into the bathroom, then transfer me onto the commode over the toilet. Many times I thought, Oh my God, a commode, my mother had to use a commode, but she was in her 80's, here I am only 58 and using a commode, what the hell is the rest of my life going to be like? It was also difficult dealing with angry overworked CNAs. Plus, being aware of all the patients who needed help but they were not getting it as soon as they needed was frustrating. But one of the most painful realizations was seeing so many patients in there with no one ever coming to visit them. I hated that the most. I was most fortunate, though, I had family and friends visiting on a regular basis.

My most favorite day was Saturdays. Kinsey would come in the morning with Dunkin Donuts coffee for Alice, me and her and we would talk, laugh and watch Phantom Gourmet and the Food Network shows. Then we would get hungry, talk about ordering out for some "good" food! God bless my dear friend Kinsey for never deserting me.

My other favorite time was once a week Donna and Diane would come for a visit with good food for dinner. Plus, they took my dirty clothes and brought them back all clean every week! This helped my daughter as she had been doing my laundry from day one as well as taking care of all my finances and paperwork…all way too much for her. But she did it all with no complaining.

Shelly and Brian went food shopping for me one day. When they came into my room with bags full of food Brian exclaimed; "Mom, I felt like we went shopping for a horse with this food we bought!" We both laughed even though I wanted to cry from embarrassment for this was not my normal healthy eating pattern. All my life, I exerted control over my eating, now that lifestyle was gone. I felt like an addict who was choosing to not be healthy, making excuses for all the food I was eating. I was especially embarrassed when Charisma returned from her LOA of 4 months. She took one look at me and said, "My God what happened to you? You were so thin when I left, how did you get so big?" Oh my God, I was devastated because I was shown my humanness, lack of control and will power which I always prided myself on. So what did I do? I buried those ugly feelings so

I could continue to eat everything I wanted. (So, I wonder; is this how drug addicts feel and what they do to continue using? My guess is probably!) Another gift of understanding I have received from this experience. We can bury and excuse anything to not get healthy and well. Again, so weird for me who loves and works diligently on being as healthy as possible, physically, mentally, emotionally and spiritually.

I decided I needed to make the best of living in the nursing home. After all, I had no home to go to, so this was to become my home. I wanted to make my experience the best I could. I did not know how long I would be there, but knew it would be longer than I would desire. Thank God I had learned many years prior, we have a choice on how we feel and then what we choose to do and experience. I had decided I wanted to live the rest of my life in peace and joy. Now what that would mean is to choose my thoughts that would support my feelings of peace and joy. It was a challenge at many times during those days, dealing with unhappy CNAs and nurses as well as patients and administration.

I loved most of my CNAs. The very first one to give me a shower became a close friend. Her name is Charisma and the name suits her very well. She gave me my first shower since my brain surgery. I loved her confidence and fun-loving personality. She put me at ease instantly. I will be forever grateful to her. I decided the best thing for me as long as I was to be here in the nursing home was to make friends with as many staff as possible. I have always believed you get what you give. So I wanted to be cared for and appreciated, so I was sure to show my appreciation for the staff's hard work.

I had roommates come and go, some crazier than others. I had made friends with Alice, the woman in the room across the hall. We would visit each other and have a few laughs One day I had a bright idea, so I went into see Alice and presented my idea. "Alice, do you want to become roommates?" I asked. She wanted to think about it, and then finally said yes. I was so excited because it meant we would know who our roommate was and could have fun on a daily basis and we did. We had many laughs and ate much food to help us get through this feeling of being in an institution that was prison-like. When I say much food, it was not the food at the nursing home. I had friends and family bring in food that brought much comfort like, animal crackers, graham crackers, cereal, and some chocolate (Alice loved her chocolate). Now I must tell you, prior to my stroke I was close to being a vegetarian—ate very few carbs, and ate mostly salads chicken, fish, tofu and occasionally eggs. I loved cottage cheese and fruit for lunches, protein shakes for breakfast. I was a very conscientious eater, not allowing extra calories to be consumed, even on holidays. Well, all hell broke loose in the nursing home after I was there a year; it was like anything goes in terms of eating. I would have cereal for breakfast every morning, graze on animal crackers during the day, have a piece of chocolate, maybe a yogurt for lunch, continue with crackers during the afternoon until the dreaded dinner. I did not like the food they served, so often I would order a grilled cheese sandwich. I ate almost no veggies and fruits, which where my staples before. I gained probably 60 lbs over the three years I was there. This was the heaviest I had ever been, including my three pregnancies.

While still in Highgate, I decided to not think about my weight. My focus was on doing what I needed to keep sane as I was waiting for an apartment to become available for me. I just knew when I moved into my own place, I would go back to my normal eating pattern and lose the weight. It was not easy to keep the focus off my weight, but I was determined to be peaceful and happy. My commitment to that helped me think better thoughts. Another tool I gained from my studies with Abraham-Hicks and the Law of Attraction. I am so grateful for all the spiritual teachers I have had during my life. I believe my soul led me to read the books I have read to deepen my knowingness of Ultimate Truth. There are too many to list here, but my gratitude and admiration is no less deep for all of them. My dream is to someday meet every one of them to thank them personally for helping me, especially during my post stroke years while in the nursing home.

Chapter 5
Abi-waiver Program

The Social Worker at the nursing home asked me one day if I would be interested in applying for a program set up for people with brain injuries. She did not know if I would be eligible but we both decided, what the heck, fill out the application and see what happens. A case manager and clinician for the ABI Waiver program came out to interview and assess my situation for eligibility. I immediately felt a connection with Ted (Case Manager) and Paula (Nurse Clinician), two dedicated and kind staff of the program who put me at ease immediately. And good news, I was approved for the ABI Waiver program, which meant I would be given all the help I needed to move into my apartment and live independently. What this meant was the program would help with buying items I needed to set up my apartment; that included furniture, appliances, linens, and kitchen items. I could not believe how much they purchased for me! Plus the Program provides aides to come help me get ready in the morning as well as get into bed in the evening. They would also clean my house and do my laundry, along with paying for my Physical and Occupational therapies. I am immensely grateful to the ABI Waiver Program for this was my full ticket to live on my own!

One day my sister called me and asked, "Would you be willing to live in Walpole?" I had been hoping to get an apartment in Foxboro since that is where my grandson was going to school. My thoughts were, if I was living in Foxboro I could help out my son, who is raising him alone, it would be a place for my grandson to come before and after school whenever necessary. I had been offered an apartment through the Foxboro Housing Authority but it was too small plus difficult for me to get into. Because I wanted out of the nursing home so desperately I was thinking maybe I could make it work. But, thank God, I was given a nudge to let it go and wait, for God was getting the perfect apartment ready for me.

So when I got that call from my sister I told her, "Of course I would live in Walpole, why?" She then proceeded to tell me she knew administration at the Walpole Housing Authority and there may be a handicapped accessible apartment available. So off we went to Walpole to fill out an emergency application. Within one week I received the call from the Housing Authority offering me the apartment! Woohoo! I was so elated I could hardly contain myself. It was the beginning of December, 2010, and I was hoping to be in my apartment for Christmas, but that was not possible for the ABI Waiver program needed to set up my services before I could move in. Of course I knew this was all for my safety, but I was so anxious to get out of the nursing home. It required much patience on my part to wait without being stressed and aggravated, as I am committed to being peaceful no matter my outside circumstances, I must admit it is not easy sometimes, but my clarity, commitment and faith are unwavering.

Chapter 6
Finally To My Apartment

It was not until March, 2011, that I was able to move into my apartment. Again, another change that was a bit scary as well as exciting. A side note; good things are worth waiting for. Although I had to wait three years for my apartment, it was most definitely worth the wait, both financially and physically it was perfect for me. I feel very safe in my apartment with amazing neighbors and aides that help me. Plus the location is very convenient, not far from where my children and grandson live, close to friends, stores, all I need. Thank you God for helping me co-create with you.

Now my challenge was to get comfortable in my new environment. Thankfully, the ABI Waiver program hired my Occupational Therapist who I worked with at the nursing home. She came to help me set up my apartment in a way to make it all easy for me to get around. She organized everything to make it accessible, for I was now going to do my own cooking. She wanted my kitchen organized for me to do just that with ease. Having Maura also added more comfort in the change from nursing home to my own home. It was a very comfortable transition indeed.

May I admit, I really wanted out of my old apartment, really wanted to buy a condominium, but never did prior to my stroke. I believe the reason was my soul knew it was not the right time to purchase, because if I had, I probably would have lost it due to my financial constraints. So another blessing from the stoke, I am in a newly renovated apartment set up just for me and surrounded by very nice people, especially my neighbors, Judy who lives in the apartment above me and Winney across the parking lot, who are the most loving positive people I have ever known.

But I must tell you, my stroke has brought me many blessings and continues to do so every day. For example, one day the agency that provides my aides sent over a woman for me to meet for my approval for her to work with me. She has truly been an angel and gift from God who helps me physically, emotionally, spiritually and mentally. I suspect if not for the stroke, we may never have met; now we are the best of friends truly loving every minute we get to spend together. Linda "gets me" like no other. Now imagine this: A friend, who never judges, loves life, loves to help people, sees the good in everyone, can see what you need and just does it without question, comes into your house with a smile, ready to work, share, listen and support.

It was not easy getting comfortable with strangers helping me shower and dress every morning. Once again I had a choice; do I want to be comfortable and peaceful or do I want to be embarrassed and stressed? Tough question, easy answer, for my commitment remains to be joyous and peaceful. So my thoughts had to focus on happy things and I mostly think funny thoughts to keep myself amused, even though I am no comedian. I can and do laugh easily, especially at myself. I have also thought many times: Oh I hope I was gentle with my kids when I dressed them! I felt like a child who was being cared for which is a strange feeling as an adult who is cognitively aware! I have decided to call myself Cleopatra for I thought; she was bathed and dressed by women in service to her, just another way to entertain myself.

One day, I found myself thinking, "I miss my breasts!" Oh really I thought back to myself. I had breast cancer twice, went through chemo and radiation the first time, then 3 years later the cancer came back so I had two mastectomies. Luckily I did not have chemo or radiation again. I decided I had been to that school, learned what I needed and did not want to go back. So now I was curious as to why after almost 6 years I was thinking about my breasts that had been removed and replaced with saline implants. Perhaps it was because I had no nipples. So, this is what I have come to understand. There are situations in our lives that we think we have dealt with emotionally when in fact quite often we bury them and pretend they do not exist or did not happen. So how could I possibly pretend I did not have two mastectomies? Well, I knew what happened on a physical level, I just did not deal with it on an emotional level. Have you ever done that, pretend there are no feelings about a certain situation? We think we can fool ourselves by burying them and pretending they do not exist. Well, I have discovered many feelings that I was unaware of. I believe it is because I am out of the madness of living life like everyone else; rushing to get ready for work, rushing to get the kids ready for school. I have found many people even rushing to go have a good time. Wow, we are an adrenalin junkie society aren't we? So now with my left side weakness, I cannot run, I must go slowly to keep myself safe from falling. Plus, I am blessed to not have to get up to go to work, although, my deepest desire is to get up and have work to do every day. I feel this way because I have been blessed to know what I love to do and I know my purpose in life. So the stroke has gifted me with the opportunity to slow down and just "be".

Chapter 7
My Fall

I had a minor setback that brought me a wonderful gift. One day, I was going to my hair stylist's house to get my hair cut and colored. Linda brought me and was helping me get up one large step onto the porch landing to get into the house.

I lost balance and down I went. Luckily nothing broke, but I did hurt my knee and could not put weight on my left leg, which is the weak one. Linda was able to help me get into the car to go back to my apartment, I called Shelly, she rushed over then she and Linda decided it be best to call an ambulance to bring me to the ER to get checked out. After x-rays showed no broken bones the ER doctor gave me an orthopedic doctor to go see for a full assessment. So I had a few tough days not being able to put my weight on my left leg. As frustrated as I was about this accident, I knew there was a gift in it as there is in every situation. I knew I needed to be patient and open to see what the gift was. For one, no bones were broken, I also learned where I went wrong in stepping up, again the power of focus, I think I lost it for a second or so and bam; down I went!

I made an appointment with the orthopedic doctor who after my exam gave me a sheet of paper with a list of physical therapists in my area. When I got home, I looked over the list and found I was immediately drawn to Norwood Physical Therapy in the town next to me. I showed the list to my occupational therapist who happened to know the physical therapy office in Walpole. A friend of hers works in that office. Now I have great respect and admiration for my occupational therapist, but my gut was telling me to go to Norwood Physical Therapy and I have learned to trust my intuition above all else as I believe it is our connection to divine and will never steer us wrong. So I called and made an appointment for an assessment that week. I must tell you, the minute I walked into the office I knew it was the right place for me for the energy was very peaceful, safe, and welcoming. Then, the physical therapist came out to greet me and lead me into the assessment room. She was very gentle, kind and thorough and assured me she could and would help me. I left there feeling quite relieved.

The next day I called to set up my appointments with Terri, who is a doctor of physical therapy as well as holds a degree in mechanical engineering—one amazing woman. The receptionist told me they do not accept my health insurance. She then asked Mike, the owner, and he told her to set up appointments with Terri for me. The first day of my PT, Mike told me they would treat me for as long as needed no problem, he also told me Terri wanted to work with me. Here I must share what I believe to be true; we attract to us like-minded people, or as the Law of Attraction states, Like attracts Like. So as I write this I realize I am giving myself a high compliment for Mike and Terri are very loving, intelligent, and caring people. Oh my, am I that good? The other important lesson is intuition usually has no logic but I was fortunate to be given the ability to see my intuition was so accurate in telling me to go to this place rather than the one Maura recommended. Now, you probably do not ever hear someone saying they enjoy going to physical therapy, but I do very much because the staff at Norwood Physical Therapy is amazing, all very kind, loving and helpful. I give credit to Mike Kane, the owner who takes pride in his office, his work, and staff as well as makes sure to greet every patient that walks through the door. And we actually have fun because most everyone is always in a good mood, including the clients, even if they are in a bit of pain. There is soul in this place which is what makes it so special and different from most places. Even though this is Mike's place of business and source of income, he cares more about the people than money, just my observation.

And a huge bonus…I can go two times per week for as long as I want no worries about insurance limitations. Really, who will allow that? Norwood Physical Therapy does with me! Now is this not a gift, get to go for support in my continued recovery for as long as I need it!

Chapter 8
What Happens In The Middle Of The Night?

Last night I woke up at 2:00 am. After I went to the bathroom, I went back to bed and found I could not go back to sleep. So I decided to just lay there and let my mind wander and see where it decided to go. I found myself thinking about many past relationships that came to a halt. Then I thought about my youngest son, who was 6 years old when his father and I decided to split. I felt as though I could feel his feelings during the years after our divorce, and then found myself crying and wondering what, if anything, that I was feeling was real. So being the one who always wants to figure human behavior and feelings out, I thought perhaps I could ask him about those years, what followed was this thought; it is his business and not yours, he will do whatever he needs to do about any feelings he may have buried. Not my job to figure anyone else out, my only job is to deal with my own damn feelings and figure my own self out!

Then my mind traveled to Bob, a man I had known for many years prior to the stroke then dated after the stroke for only 4 months, but thought for sure he was "the one." But unfortunately he did not feel the same way. I found myself crying once again over the lost relationship, plus hating to have to feel the immense sadness and not able to talk myself out of the uncomfortable feeling of deep sadness.

I think I finally was able to relax, calm down enough to go to sleep around 4:00am. So here is the lesson I learned from those two dark hours in the middle of the night:

We wake for a reason at this time; it is quiet so it affords us the opportunity of quiet to allow feelings to surface and think. I truly thought I had resolved all my issues with past relationships and situations. But this middle-of-the-night experience showed me I had not completely resolved those issues. I think what I did do was intellectualize in the past to keep myself from feeling the deep pain of my situations. So now what I believe to be true is we all have deep feelings that we believe have been discarded when in fact they have been deeply buried, but are still alive in our bodies. They are so very toxic and need to be released otherwise will cause sickness in our bodies and minds. It is so easy to not realize the feelings are there because we are all so busy to keep occupied or we turn to something either legal or illegal to keep feelings buried. In my case while in the nursing home I used food so I would not have to feel the sadness of my physical condition as well as not having a home to go to.

I have now made a commitment to myself to pay attention to my feelings and if a negative one creeps in I acknowledge it, try to understand it, cry if I need to then let it go knowing the universe will take it on. I then try to get to a better thought, knowing all is well and congratulate myself for facing a nasty feeling and releasing it. If this sounds easy or too simple it is not. It takes a true commitment to work through any negative feelings to let them leave our bodies. I want to be healthy and peaceful to understand and accept the work involved to be there.

Chapter 9
Alone and Crying

Last night as I watched two movies about lost loved ones, I found myself crying my eyes out. I felt so lonely on a Saturday night with no one to be with. I just let myself cry hard, something I don't usually do. For some reason, I thought it was important to let myself cry without thinking about it or judging it good or bad, just cry. When the crying stopped, that is when I decided to think about it. I wanted to know why I was crying, where it came from and why I allowed it. I find myself very consistent in wanting to understand the reasons of feelings and situations.

This is what I thought; I was crying over lost loves, the ending of all my relationships with the men I thought I would be with, or settled down with in a committed relationship. For example, my two husbands; never in a million years as a kid did I think I would ever get divorced once, never mind twice! And when I found a man I felt a strong connection with, I felt we would make the relationship work, but obviously they were not meant to be. Now as I was thinking about these relationships, I realized I did not mourn or grieve the loss of them, I did not feel the sadness, anger, frustration, all the feelings a normal human goes through with grief and loss. I guess my style is to just not look at the negative feelings and look forward to the future and new, don't look back.

I now understand it very important to face and feel our feelings, no matter how difficult for they are there for a reason. Because I have decided to face them—not bury them with an addiction like eating as I did in the nursing home—I came out happier and prouder of myself for facing the shit and not breaking. I actually felt stronger for releasing a weight I had been carrying without realizing, the negative buried feelings.

Do I still feel lonely? Sometimes yes I do. Now I know I can get through it by feeling and moving through to my Trusting Place, where I believe ALL IS WELL AND IN PERFECT ORDER.

Chapter 10
Trip To The Pacemaker Clinic

Once a year I must go to the pacemaker clinic at Mass General Hospital. That is where I had my brain surgery after the stroke, as well as a pacemaker implanted just under the skin near my heart. I do remember being brought to the operating room for the procedure. I was not scared but I remember not feeling overjoyed with another procedure, so I went to my trusting place which helped me stay calm knowing all was well. There was no pain but I remember a tugging feeling inside where they placed the pacemaker. What I later realized is the tugging was the connection being made to my heart so the pacemaker could do its thing.

There is so much I do not remember about the hospital since I did not need to know where everything was, but as my daughter pointed out as we were walking to the pacemaker clinic, she knew every square inch of the hospital. Then Shelly pointed out to me the bench outside where she and Christopher sat and prayed while I was being operated on. At that moment, I was overcome with sadness for what my children had to go through. Another reminder here, I am the fortunate one. I am not reliving that scene, nor have any awareness of the seriousness of my condition. But yesterday as Shelly was telling me what she knew and experienced, it was like I was experiencing it myself and I was overcome with emotions for my kids. I hated they had to go through this crisis. I talked to God in my head to try to not let Shelly see I was ready to cry. No, I wanted to scream! But as usual, I contained myself, went to my trusting place and went into the clinic. We were pleasantly surprised we did not have a long wait, last year our wait was almost an hour.

Now as much as I look completely composed on the outside, I do feel a bit anxious when here, but shush don't tell anyone, please, God forbid anyone should know I am human with feelings of fear. I only want to show my good side, my strength, my positive upbeat side, my everything-is-well side. Now guess what? I do get scared, pissed, frustrated, and judgmental. Yes, I'm totally human and this is what has been more difficult than any physical limitations I may have.

During the pacemaker testing, the woman conducting the test at one point told me she was going to try something and wanted me to tell her if I felt it in a bad way. So in my usual way, I just tried to ignore the whole procedure but no hiding for me with Shelly there watching my every move. I was feeling a bit lightheaded but didn't want to say. I think Shelly said something and after hearing Shelly's voice the nurse knew she did not need to go any further. I started to breathe easier until Shelly got upset with the results showing I had some A-fib episodes. The nurse was not concerned as they were very short episodes and not too many. Again, I was feeling my daughter's negative feelings;

I just let her have them, hoping she would calm down. I shared my thoughts with her; "I do have a pacemaker to keep my heart in correct rhythm as well as my medication, so I am perfectly fine."

The other realization I had was; I have very little recollection of what I experienced during my stay at the hospital, perhaps this was a way for me to feel the importance of what happened to me. But I did not want to feel the pain Christopher and Shelly experienced due to my health issues. Wow, I know they both have PTSD from this experience. God bless them, may they overcome their pain and get to their trusting places!

Chapter 11
Uncle Fred & Carolyn's Wedding

I have had many people ask me how I keep smiling and happy. As I write this it has been almost six years since my stroke. Yesterday I was honored to be able to attend the wedding of my uncle, my father's youngest brother who is 81 years young. The room where he had the reception was filled with my siblings, aunts and uncles, all my cousins, their spouses and children. The room was so filled with love, I almost burst. I was reminded; I come from love, surrounded by love and am filled with love in my heart and soul. So how can I not be smiling and happy? I have been blessed with a very special loving extended family along with the ability to see the positive gift in every situation — even though it may take a minute or two. Watching my uncle dance with his new wife, singing to her while looking at her with loving, grateful eyes was an experience I will never forget. It filled my heart with such joy and hope that someday I would find my true love. I know he is out there and I am waiting patiently, well sometimes not too patiently; I am human after all and do love immediate gratification. Like most of us humans, we want what we want (Right?)!

My uncle had been married to one of my favorite fun loving women in the world, whom everyone in the family, including my dad loved. She passed before my father and I know how devastated my uncle was. They truly were a perfect couple. So when I found out he was dating another wonderful woman, I was elated. My aunt Edie introduced them. I believe she intuitively knew they were perfect for each other, and she was right on!!!

It only made sense to me that they would marry and spend the rest of their days in this loving, joyous relationship. I love looking daily at their wedding picture I have sitting on my table next to my alter in my living room. It is a reminder to me what I will soon have. Thank you Uncle Fred and Carolyn for your loving example of a healthy beautiful relationship in our senior years!

Chapter 12
What I Have Learned In The Past Six Years

I have discovered so much after the stroke. I want to share with you to give you some food for thought. Please remember only you hold your truth, no one can tell you how to feel or what to believe for you carry inside you all the wisdom and answers you need to exist in this life.

It is my honor to share what I have discovered what is true for me.

☐ Experience is the best teacher; you can learn from text-books and gain knowledge   from others, but only with experience do you know something fully.

☐ Quite often we think we "know" something, but do not apply it in our actions. For example, prior to the stroke, I learned about The Law of Attraction. I taught it and thought I was using it, but I wasn't fully trusting what I wanted would come to me. Then I had the stroke and have experienced manifesting what I desire on a regular basis. It's about the little things.

□ I am a born teacher, I love sharing information and I am a leader. Perhaps another way to put this is I don't keep my mouth shut. Whenever I am around people, I feel as though I have an audience to speak to—whether they know it or like it or not. I must pray for these poor people who happen to be in my presence.

□ I am fully committed to my life purpose every day. My desire is to share in a bigger way. I love an audience and desire to speak to very large audiences. I now feel ready for the big time! Prior to the stroke I was not ready, was unable to see how it could happen. Now that I have found my trusting place, the how does not matter, I know God will show me how and when.

□ Other than my three magical children, the stroke has been my biggest gift; it has taught me so many things as well as given me a platform to serve my life purpose in the bigger way I desire.

□ Our children are our teachers, not the other way around. As parents we think we are older and know more than our children. We may have been on the earth longer, but that does not mean we know better as we like to think and believe. All three of my children have taught me about myself by bringing to light what I was doing. For instance, my oldest was 6 or 7 when I was threatening a punishment on him if he did something. His immediate response was, "No you won't do that mommy because you never do!" Oh, what a wake-up call I got at that moment. He was so right; I did not realize I use to threaten without follow-through. That stopped me dead in my tracks and made sure from that day on I never threatened. I also made fewer rules so I could follow through on consequences.

Another great example is from my youngest when he was around 12. We were out to dinner and I was sharing with him something negative about a friend, something I did not like that she was doing. He stopped me by saying, "Mom, I wonder what you say about me to other people." Wow another big wake up call. What this so poignantly taught me was to never speak about a person in a negative way to another human being. If I have a problem with someone, resolve it either by talking with them or on my own by writing or talking with a therapist to help me get out of the negativity.

I now will not talk about a person that is not in my presence, unless it is something I would say to their face, it is only fair and just in my mind.

Also my daughter at 15 years old gave me a great lesson. My ex-husband and I were going through a tough time and I was very sad about our situation. One night I was sharing with Shelly how sad I was; she responded with, "Mom, you are going to have a best friend one day in me, but I cannot be that right now at 15, it will probably happen when I am around 25." So the lesson here is; our children need us to be parents not friends. We cannot look to our children to be our friends or social outlets; we must have our own peer groups and our children need their own friends.

☐ Attitude is everything.

☐ The Law of Attraction is very complex but is REAL. Actually the Law is easy; the complexity is in the use and understanding of it. I may not be the expert of it, but I have discovered how it works for me. This is my understanding: We co-create with God/The Universe—we have a job and the universe has its job. My job is threefold: 1. Be clear on what I desire, 2. Believe that it already exists, and 3. Have faith and patience to allow it to come to me, by trusting God/The Universe will show me the how's of getting it, by paying attention to the inspired action steps without thought:

☐ Miracles happen every day if you allow yourself to see and experience them.

☐ Confidence is one of the biggest keys to success. My confidence has helped me obtain what I want; one example is starting my coaching business. I knew I wanted my own business but wasn't sure what it was so I set forth to discover what my business would be by reading, journaling and talking to people. When a friend introduced me to coaching I realized, This is it, I am a coach and have been my whole life, so I started my coaching business while working full time. And as my confidence grew, clients and opportunities came to me, so that I could leave my full time job and work solely in my business. I have no formal degrees; but I have confidence in myself along with faith in God/The Universe to help me help myself.

☐ How to work through fear. I have never been a fear-based person. After the stroke, I noticed a fear of walking. I was afraid of falling or being alone. I realized if I did not face my fears, I would keep myself in prison, for that is what fears do. So I have learned how to keep myself safe; when walking, I must only focus on my walking which gives new meaning to the funny saying, you can't chew gum and walk at the same time– truth. There is so much we do unconsciously, but I must be aware at all times, in the moment, to keep myself safe.

☐ How to ask for and allow myself to receive help. I see the gift it gives to others; to receive from another is to definitely gift them. People love to help and while allowing people to help me, I see the good feeling looks on their faces. They feel proud of themselves and it makes me so happy to see them feeling so good.

☐ Balancing our humanness and divinity (Ego/Soul) is difficult but not impossible. Our soul is our connection to God/The Universe and carries all our wisdom, love, understanding, compassion, kindness, joy, truth and fun. Our egos carry fear and fear will try to sabotage our happiness. Now there is a difference, however, between caution and fear; caution keeps us safe and in the moment, fear holds us back. For example, I am cautious when I walk and drive. When I feel fear, I will not walk or drive and I am able to do both when I remove my fear.

☐ Our hearts will never steer us wrong.

☐ The importance of recognizing and paying attention to our intuition.

☐ We cannot help someone who does not want to be helped.

☐ I celebrate being human while at other times hate it.

☐ What we believe becomes our reality. You may want something and feel the desire very strongly but, if you do not believe you can have it for any reason; you will probably not receive it.

☐ I believe it would be helpful that the medical community understood the power of faith, love and patience. And doctors cannot save a person who is ready to die (our souls are more powerful than the doctors).

☐ Love is the most powerful force in the world and it needs to start with oneself.

☐ Everything happens for a reason and it's usually for our highest good even though it may not appear that way.

☐ We each have our own way of living and we each are correct for ourselves.

☐ We cannot tell anyone something they don't already know.

☐ Even though I feel I have been blessed with access to my soul wisdom, I don't feel I am any better than anyone else on earth.

☐ There will always be mysteries in life, enjoy the excitement of that by accepting we will not know everything we want.

☐ Patience, Patience, Patience; I remember when I was young being told "Patience is a virtue." What I understand now is patience allows us to slow down, see miracles, focus, and appreciate all we have.

☐ Faith. Without faith, I would not be writing this book or living as fully as I do.

☐ Belief in oneself.

☐ Respect what others believe or have to say, but don't own it if it does not resonate.

☐ What you believe you receive.

☐ Love is the most powerful force in the world.

I believe the stroke has served me well in my evolution on earth. Although there has been much pain and disruption due to the stroke, the gifts have been greater, as I have listed above. My stroke has made me a better person by allowing me to become who I truly am. I am experiencing fully that I am more than my body; I am peace, love, joy, compassion, understanding, fun, forgiveness, courage, kindness and wisdom. And most importantly, I know I am a child of God/The Universe as we all are. I am no better or worse than another living person on this beautiful planet. But I must admit; I feel very blessed to have the awareness that I do.

YOU are just like me, at the soul-level. I am just here to remind you what you may have forgotten. Stop for a moment now, close your eyes and feel what is in your heart, not your mind. You are BEAUTIFUL; you are perfect just as you are. Now if your mind is playing tricks on you, take one word – LOVE – now think that in your mind, repeat it until you can feel it in your heart. Our minds are a beautiful computer for us to work with. It is time for us to learn the operating system to allow our minds to work for us, not against us.

A thought just came to me; we truly receive what we believe. No one can tell you how to live your life or the steps to success. Only if you BELIEVE what a person is telling you can you make it happen for you. This is why I did not want to write a step process book. If something resonates with you from another source, then it is probably true for you. Please know you are the CEO of your life, you are creating it and running it the way you choose. Congratulations on your big position!

Chapter 13
Our Wants

In case you have not noticed I am very spiritually based, I do see things from a spiritual perspective. Again, the stroke has afforded me this opportunity, given the time I have had to follow my passion, which is spirituality. Equally as important, I have also loved human behavior since I was a little girl. So I watch and listen to how people talk and behave. Through this wonderful pastime for me, I have come to the realization that we all want similar things in life:

- To be heard.
- To be understood.
- To be validated.
- To be soothed.
- To love and be loved.
- To feel good; physically and mentally.
- To be happy and at peace.
- To be wealthy – worry free of money.
- To be okay with our emotions.
- To feel safe.

Chapter 14
The Ego and Divine Support

Another observation; I have watched many egos running the show or in battle with other egos. But most do not understand it is their ego running the show because their point feels so logical and makes perfect sense to their logical mind. This is ego talking, though, not the heart.

For example, I have an Occupational Therapist and a Chiropractor who specializes in brain/body connections helping me get my left arm and hand working again. They both have given me exercises to help create neuropaths in my brain. So after making the mistake of telling each about the other, each of their reactions was interesting. I foolishly thought each of them would be happy that I had the support that I needed. Instead, their egos wanted to be the right one, the one to win with the perfect answer. My conclusion is their egos wanted to be right, have the one right answer to help me, but I do believe their souls want the best for me and are doing their best to provide total support to me. I love and appreciate them both and know in my heart they are giving me their very best. So lesson learned; keep my mouth shut, don't share everything because what I share is put out to be judged by egos.

I am a very open and honest woman who loves to share all that is happening in my life that feels good and exciting. I understand not everyone wants to know what I have to share. And God bless them for helping me see and understand this. We are all unique and special in how we think and do things. As my mother use to tell me: "variety is the spice of life!" An amazingly wise, wonderful woman she was. She has been gone from earth for over two years now. I so wish I could talk with her here in person to let her know how much I love and appreciate her. I know she has been with me in spirit through this amazing time in my life.

As a matter of fact, I know I have much divine support that is getting me through this physically, emotionally, and spiritually challenging period of my life. I cannot see or hear them, but I am fortunate to just know they are all with me. I have no logical proof, just a knowingness which is all I have needed to get me through. Fortunately, I don't get flustered when I have no logical proof for those that ask me, but quite often Spirit will put a thought in my head that I can tell the person that may make them see the possibility and perhaps give them something to think about. I love giving inspiration that causes others to think.

I don't feel I need to prove anything to anyone. There is no one right way. Each and every one of us is right in where we are and what we are doing. There are many paths to bring you to where you want to go; we each pick the path that is right for us at any given moment.

I have discovered so much after the stroke. I want to share with you only to give you some food for thought. Please remember only you hold your truth, no one can tell you how to feel or what to believe for you carry inside you all the wisdom and answers you need to exist in this life. It is my honor to share what I have discovered what is true for me.

This book probably would not have been written had it not been for the stroke which has actually served me well providing many gifts. I pray this stroke will serve you as well as my prayer includes that you do not need to go through this type of crisis in order to become wiser or enlightened. You will notice I quite often do not call the stroke, MY stroke; I call it THE stroke because it does not belong to me or define me. I believe it came to me in service to all of us and this is my story. I pray it helps you in whatever way it serves you best.

We are so much more than our bodies. I am so grateful to know this. If I were just my body my guess is I would not be as happy as I am. As Dr. Maya Angelou once said, "In every cloud there is a rainbow and that rainbow is our soul in God."

My parents served my Higher Purpose. I use to complain about my childhood not being what I wished it had; I guess I was playing the victim role seeing only the negatives and not the blessings that filled my life. Thankfully I changed it around before I turned 40. And now I would rather see how they served my soul and not my body, although they took very good care of my total well-being, I am most grateful for all they gave me. I've learned to honor, respect and admire all days, experiences and situations here on earth and there is no doubt in my mind my parents are watching over me every moment of my life and helping me go on.

I desire to help you appreciate all you have right now in your life, no matter how small or difficult. Everything serves a higher purpose, something most of us are unaware. For example, the stroke served me in seeing my purpose on earth and provided the forum for me to serve it. Prior to the stroke, I was very busy making money spending my time not only working in my business but also worrying how I could make it grow and do only what I loved to do. I left little time for rest and relaxation although I used to teach my students the importance of that, especially while growing and running your own business. I spoke it but I was not totally living it.

Now I am living only from joy by first knowing what makes me happy then trusting it will come to me by being in my trusting place. I know I know this sounds ridiculous, no logic on how this can be possible. But I have learned to become worry-free, knowing all is in perfect order and with God all things are possible. So being in my trusting place is also allowing me deep faith that all is well and in perfect order.

We are so much more than our bodies and I am so grateful to know this. I believe my knowledge of this has helped me recover from the stroke. Our beliefs create our reality, and every situation in our life is perfect. Once again, as Dr. Maya Angelou says: "There is a rainbow in every cloud and that rainbow is our soul in God." I call it my trusting place, where all is well and perfect within me. It is within you also. You just need to be still and feel the peace inside your heart and soul, not your mind.

Chapter 15
Women's Issues

Having been a woman my whole life has provided me insight about us females. We tend to be a bit more insecure than men, not on everything but on a select list of things. We have not been taught how to love and appreciate ourselves, mostly only to care for others. Now I believe it to be true that women do tend to be nurturers, but we do not nurture ourselves for fear we will appear selfish.

Oh SELFISH, I could write a book on that word and our ridiculous connotations of it. When you hear the word "selfish" what is the first thing you think? Narcissistic, only care about themselves, not caring about others feelings or needs, only their own. I like to use the word self-care in place of selfish as it feels more positive. (thank you Cheryl Richardson for exposing that term!). Since the stroke, I have had to learn to pay close attention to what I need; mostly in order to keep myself safe. Plus our needs are on the human level; at the soul level we need nothing. Oh the complexity of trying to discern what comes from ego and what is coming from my soul: And my discernment was necessary so I could continuously move forward in my journey of recuperating.

There were many times I just wanted to give up because it can feel all so difficult, having to wear a brace on my leg due to foot drop, having to walk slowly and focused to keep myself safe, wearing a brace on my arm and hand at night, to keep my hand in proper position, not being able to use my left arm and hand as usual Without the brace my hand closes and I do not want it to stay permanently closed. Oh and having to use a commode in my bedroom is quite embarrassing. I go to Physical therapy twice a week and Occupational therapy once a week. Plus every day I exercise my hand and arm to get it working again, please God! I am tired just writing about this. I feel like a whiney little girl and I do not like this feeling.

Chapter 16
Overcoming Loneliness

Today was one of those lonely days for me. It is Sunday and I am alone, which gives me too much time to think and feel. It was easy for me to first feel sad and lonely. After giving logical credit to those thoughts and feelings, I then decided I wanted to feel better by not sitting in poop.

So let me tell you what I do when I get like this, I look at the fact I am alive and have a purpose! I feel very blessed to have this feeling. Then, I think about my beautiful future coming at me.

I feel blessed to have three wonderful children and caring friends and an amazing grandson all of whom I adore. I can think clearly as well as speak well. I live independently. I can cook for myself. I can walk. I can dress myself. But most importantly, I CAN LOVE! I feel the amazing amount of love in my heart, so I love to give my love to everyone I meet. For I firmly believe, only love is real, all the rest is an illusion. When I have the honor of talking with another through my heart, it is glorious to watch that person smile and get happy or relieved. My job is to help people see who they truly are by my being who I am, my soul, not my ego. How glorious that I have all this awareness! Do I have all my answers? NO, but I do know what I know; who I am, my purpose in life, the meaning of my life, I know God is real, alive and everywhere, I know we are all spiritual beings having a very human experience, I know there is no bad soul, only souls who have forgotten who they are, this I have learned from Neale Donald Walsch's book THE LITTLE SOUL AND THE SUN. I wish every person could read this book for it helps us see why some people seem very bad to us. All of Neale's books are life transforming for me and millions of other human beings.

I mostly love my ability to have an open mind, heart and soul. I love that I have learned to receive; this is something many of us, especially women, have some difficulty with. For to receive from another is like saying to that person; "I trust you and value who you are, what you are saying and doing." And this is a confidence builder, a way to make another feel valued and purposeful. I believe if we don't feel purposeful, we have difficulty living, for we may think there is no reason to be alive or know what to do. Actually, we have nothing to DO, we are here to BE. After all, we are human beings not human doings. But our ego and society tells us we must be doing something in order to be valuable, they think our mere existence is not enough, when in fact it is more than enough!

As I am watching so many women not happy and some seeming scared, I am reminded everything I see is about me and not the other. So the two questions I must ask myself are what am I unhappy about and what scares me? I must admit two things quickly pop into my mind; I am unhappy about my situation; body weakness and feelings of being alone, no partner not enough work that I love and too much time on my hands. What scares me? Maybe I am wrong about my future. But in all honesty, I know that is my ego trying to trick me from listening to my soul—where I carry all my wisdom and faith. For my soul knows my future is extremely bright, filled with all my heart's desires: an amazing partner, career, friends, classes, financial abundance, speaking engagements, book signings and most important abundant health and well-being. Which means my body is back to allowing me to walk, dance, and run as desired, showering and dressing on my own, ability to carry things with both arms and hands, and write with my left hand as I use to. I just watched a show that highlighted two women that were dealing with amputated legs and getting accustomed to walking with prosthetic legs. As I was listening to their stories and feeling their courage, this is what crossed my mind; they are so much braver than me, better than me because, I did not lose my legs, I only have left side weakness, they are dealing with so much more than me, my story is not nearly as remarkable as theirs. I decided to share my thoughts and feelings about this with my dear friend that evening. She told me her feelings about what I told her and she showed me, we all are remarkable in what we are dealing with in life. No one is better than another, it is all relative.

So my message to you; your situation is the perspective you give it. No need to compare, we are each unique individuals having our own experiences that are valid, important and meaningful. You have the right to feel whatever you feel and if you don't like how you are feeling you can change it with your thoughts and perspective. Plus, everything is relative.

Chapter 17
Thanksgiving

Thanksgiving has always been my favorite holiday as an adult, as a child I did love the wonder and magic of Christmas, but I also loved Thanksgiving. In our house growing up, it was crazy-packed, not with people, but with food. I grew up in an Italian family and our holidays reflected the food of the Italian culture. Every part of Italy has its own culture as do we here in America. It all depends on your geographic location, what you do and what you will be eating. So in my family on every holiday was my mother, father, older and younger brothers, my grandparents, my mother's parents and my baby sister. I loved every one of them more than they will ever know, not that I acted that way all the time, but I especially loved holidays when we were all together. As an Italian woman, I love family and being with family is the most enjoyable thing I can do, that includes my aunts, uncles and cousins.

As the saying goes, some people live to eat and some eat to live. I had always been one who ate to live. But on Thanksgiving I lived to eat!

Now let me tell you about our Thanksgiving meals. First we started with antipasto which included, all Italian

…ses, olives and relish tray and of course much bread. Once we finished the first course, and out the pasta, which was usually lasagna or ravioli. would clear the table for the main course of Turkey the usual trimmings. By the time we finished the first courses, most of us felt how in heck could we possibly turkey now? But my mother did such a wonderful job of ooking it all and it was Thanksgiving so we had to eat the turkey!

One of the reasons I love Thanksgiving so much is, I love turkey and all the vegetables that go with it plus, I love to feed people and I find this dinner easy to prepare and serve. I just love seeing everyone at the table anxiously waiting for the food.

After my divorce but prior to the stroke, I had in my dining room the furniture from my childhood which held such sentimental values because my father made the glass topped wrought iron dining table which I found most beautiful. As a kid when I would clean it, I found myself cherishing the work my father put into it. I was so proud of him and all his abilities. So to have this table surrounded by my children, my very dear friend Bruce and his girlfriend, Linda was just sheer joy for me. It did not matter the work or cost to put into this holiday, for to have my kids with me was all that mattered. I did do antipasto because my kids loved it, but I skipped out on the pasta, sorry Nana, I just knew it was too much and I tried to keep it as simple as possible. I made sure to have the food that my people loved including the deserts.

So to spend three years in the nursing home without being able to cook, especially my favorite holiday, was a bit sad for me. But my kids did come in to have dinner with me. I hope they know how much that helped me get through the holidays.

So of course my first Thanksgiving in my new apartment was huge for me. But the big issue and problem was I could not do it the way I did prior to stroke. That was frustrating and sad but I WAS HOME OUT OF THE NURSING HOME IN MY OWN APARTMENT! And that is mostly what I was focusing on, the joy of being on my own. So another issue was Brian was not here and I did not have the room to have Bruce and Linda over. Bruce was my significant other for over 7 years and after our breakup we became good friends as we will always be, we accept the fact we love each other but cannot live together, so we settle for being friends. He has been a big part of my life and we all love having him around since he keeps us laughing and totally entertained with his antics!

It was November 2012 and I hosted a Thanksgiving meal as I had always done prior to the stoke. I was so excited to have the kids coming over and my dear friend Kinsey, only Brian would be missing because he was in Afghanistan, so we were hoping to be able to Skype with him. What was so different is due to my left sided weakness, I was unable to lift and do things in the kitchen as I had before. I needed to get over the sadness of that, so I decided to think about how happy and blessed I was to be home and making one of my favorite meals for a favorite holiday. Shelly came to help and do what was difficult for me. Again I was reminded how I would love to have my man with me helping with all this. I was still single but ALIVE and for that I was most grateful! I seem to get these constant reminders of looking at the good in every situation in order to be happy and joyous, for that is my choice so my thoughts must support that choice to be what I desire to be! We are at choice on how we want to feel and be. It is our thoughts that create our feelings. Here is how that goes; first we must be clear on what we want, second we must be committed to it, third believe it exists (for example, you are already who you want to be), then it requires patience to allow it to be, or if you are desiring something, patience, focus and belief is what it takes to allow it to come to your reality. This is not a written rule or the only WAY to accomplish anything; it is what has worked for me.

My desire for this whole book is to share my story and experiences with the hope there may be something you take away from it that is positive for you in your life. I have realized through my experience I have developed my own step process and would love to help others design their own step process in creating the reality of their dreams.

Chapter 18
Life Can Be Difficult

Life can be difficult especially when we are unaware of how it all works and that we are spiritual beings having a human experience. And as humans we all have our coping mechanisms—healthy and unhealthy as well as legal and illegal—to get through the difficult times. During my whole life I have used a few coping mechanisms, thank God they are legal but not always healthy and good for me.

I used food as my coping mechanism during my three year stay in the nursing home following my stroke and that is my story.

There have been many challenges to face since I had the stroke. One of the biggest is facing my negative feelings.

I recognize how I have evolved over the years, how much I have learned and changed. My belief is we all can change if we so desire but we also automatically evolve as we continue to live on this beautiful earth, that's just the way it is. Now I want to tell you, my childhood was not bad but like everything in life, it was far from perfect. I use to feel my parents did not support me, I was angry with them for so many things and I use to blame them for my feeling so miserable. The day came when I was in my therapist's office and she started to complain about my parents. It felt awful and I immediately stopped her and said; "I am an adult now and can live my life how I choose, I do not want to put blame on my parents for my discomfort!" Wow, that saying is so true, I can say anything I want about my family good or bad but YOU better NEVER say anything bad! This was another huge wakeup call for me in realizing I was taking full responsibility for my life.

Another kick in the pants I got from a different therapist was a question she asked me in one session; "Do you like to complain?" Oh man what a shot that was to hear. On that day I decided I did not want to ever complain again about anything! I felt completely embarrassed and exposed that day, there was no place to hide. So I started in a new direction; bypass any negative feeling and look at something positive. Perhaps this was the start of my spiritual practice and outlook.

What I have now come to understand, I was burying my negative feelings like I was an addict taking a drug to not feel anything. Because, in order to feel my feelings, I would have to do something with them and the only thing I knew to do was complain which just kept me stuck in the negativity. I was not taught it was okay to feel anything other than good or happy. Since the stroke, I have come to realize our feelings get buried, but they never go away, they lay dormant in our body somewhere. We need to face all our feelings, walk through them which helps them dissipate. I have always wanted to jump to the positive in any situation because that would make me feel better; I made that my drug of choice. I do not like talking about any difficult situation because I do not want to give it any energy. I like looking and talking about the solution, it feels better and helps bring it forward quicker.

Perhaps this is why I enjoy being a coach, to help people gain clarity on the solutions and develop action steps to obtain their goals.

Chapter 19
My Trusting Place

So what and where is the Trusting Place? It is the place in our heart and soul that is connected with God. It is where our faith takes over our ego. It is the place of extreme peace. It is our heaven on earth. It is where we carry all our wisdom; it is our worry-free space. I had been searching for it almost my whole life and finally found it after the stroke. This is one big reason to be grateful for the stroke although I have myriad reasons for my gratitude. As you read through this book, I hope you will see my reasons and how my perspective works to keep me thriving to this very moment six years later.

As I write this, I am now in a new phase of my journey. For all of us each day is a new phase, so please understand I am no different than you, all I am doing is sharing what I am feeling and going through as I continue to live my life. My license was revoked after I had the stroke. I admit it was uncomfortable receiving that statement from the RMV, I felt sad but totally understood. This was another reality check for me that I was not viewed as physically whole. I have had to work diligently every day to not succumb to that view, while still accepting my physical limitations to keep myself safe. My limitations are left side weakness; I walk with a quad cane for balance and at this time, I do not have use of my left arm or hand, so I do everything with my right arm and hand. I have believed from the beginning I would be completely healed gaining all strength back on my left side. This takes a commitment on my part to exercise every day, go to Physical and Occupational therapy twice a week for each and continuously keep a positive attitude. While that is not possible 24/7, I believe I am doing the best I can.

I decided I would get my license back as soon as I possibly could, so I did what I had to do to get it back. There were a few hoops I had to go through, but nothing was going to stop me from driving. My need for independence trumped everything, for it is a priority of mine so I may live my life as fully as I can without needing to depend on others too often.

A side note here, I believe we are meant to live on earth interdependently; we are all here to help one another while helping ourselves. This has been a huge lesson for me, and one that I believe most do not understand fully, especially stubborn independents such as myself! Thank you again for the stroke and the opportunity to learn and experience so much.

So once I had my license, I needed a car. It turns out purchasing a car was another long process. With determination I did and purchased a beautiful car that is perfect for me right now. So here is what is challenging; I wanted my license and a car so I could go out on my own whenever I wanted but now I am scared! Plus I am angry with myself for being scared. I never want anyone to see I have any fear, so I do my best to hide it and cry in silence hoping no one will ever know I have one iota of fear.

I share this with you in hopes you gain some acceptance of any negative feelings you may have. It is all part of being alive, a reminder, if you will, we are living and experiencing. Yes, sometimes it is not fun, but wait just a minute and it will and can change.

The reason I felt scared was due to the fact I would be going out to places by myself for the first time in over 5 years. In my soul I knew it would be fine, I just needed to do it, experience it and feel the freeing feeling of it. Truly independent for the first time since the stroke was a bigger deal than I had imagined. Another lesson learned, actually one I seem to keep learning over and over so that hopefully one day I get it; we are spiritual beings having a human experience. Without being in a human body, we could not experience our spiritual selves. This means we experience the all of being human; the good, the bad, and the ugly.

But I have come to understand it is all good, even when it stinks and feels awful because we are alive and serving our highest good. If you read Neale Donald Walsch's book, Conversations with God Book One, you will get what I am saying here. Thank you, Neale, for writing all your books that have transformed my life for the better.

Chapter 20
The Mall

My very first outing in my car by myself was to the mall in my town. After I worked through the fear of going out by myself for the first time, I got into my car, drove to the mall and here is what happened. I got out, locked the door, walked over to the crosswalk to cross the street part of the lot to go into the mall. A very nice woman in a grey car stopped at the crosswalk and waved me to go across. Because I walk so slowly, I told her to go first but she refused and kept waving for me to go across. Once I reached the other side, I turned to thank her and she yelled out, "No problem!" Now as I was approaching the handicap accessible door a woman jumped to the knob to open the door and told me she would hold the door open until I got in. She also shared that she had a special needs daughter and understood what I was going through. I made it into the mall and found a bench to sit on to rest for a minute. I felt so joyous and thankful that I started to cry. While I was sitting there my phone rang, it was Christopher, my oldest; I answered but was still crying. He was concerned and kept asking me what is wrong, Mom? I told him I was crying tears of joy because of what I just did and all the help I got from the very kind and patient women. I was able to convince him I was perfectly fine, God bless his heart for all his concern for me. I then got up and walked to the nail salon to get a mani-pedi—which turned into another experience of very kind, gentle and understanding women.

Okay women, when are we going to get how powerful our love and patience can be for others? Plus, we need to be loving, kind and patient with ourselves first, another mission of mine to help us understand our feminine power. We don't have to be like men, although I deeply love and appreciate men. Let us learn from our differences, honor, respect and celebrate them; it's part of what makes the world go round.

After I finished at the salon I successfully made it back into my car and drove home with the biggest smile on my face. I was feeling full of gratitude and excitement with my freedom and accomplishments.

As I continue to go places by myself, I continuously experience what I believe to be true: God has placed angels on my path to help me get in and out of buildings easily and safely. My heart is full of joy as I write this truth for myself. It is so amazing to experience these miracles every day.

Miracles happen to those who believe because what you believe you can see. Now how can this happen? Do you know what a belief is? It is a stream of thoughts you have been told or read, they feel logical and make sense so you incorporate them into your belief system. So if a belief is not working for you, you just create one that will work. Develop a stream of thoughts that feels good, say them out loud every day for 30 days or longer and perhaps you have developed a belief that will bring joy to you. I offer no guarantees here, but it is worth a try. What have you got to lose? For example, I believed I would get my license and a car and it all happened in time. I keep believing and visioning while waiting for it to come into my reality. I don't have to force anything, in my patience I am given inspired action steps.

Chapter 21
Talking With Friends

Let me start with I love myself and I love my life; this is a mantra I learned from my coach, thank you Max Ryan. I say this affirmation among others every day in the morning. It has opened up my heart to see what I truly feel. Today, I realized how much I appreciate all I have learned in my life so far. So right now as I am writing I am approaching the young age of 65, I know some think it to be old, but I see it as only a number. So why do I love my life and where I am at right now? I am better able to see things from my heart and soul most of the time; of course my ego loves to nudge me now and then to remind me I am still very human and alive! This I choose to celebrate and feel much gratitude. As I walk through my days, I find myself thinking and saying often, but I am alive and have more living to do, how glorious. This feels so much better than, Oh my God, this sucks that it is difficult for me to walk and use my left arm and hand plus I don't like my pants feeling tight…but who cares…I AM ALIVE THANK YOU GOD!

When I am speaking with people, I love hearing them with my heart, especially the ones who speak with their heart. They remind me how much I have learned…too much to write in this book. Now another very good friend who has helped me create my book once told me, "I want you to share more of you in your book, I want your wisdom to be out there," My first reaction was, "But I don't want to bore them or tell them what to do!" So if I am getting too wordy, I can blame it on Travis (He he).

I have come to realize every generation thinks their way is the "right" way of doing things and then get frustrated in watching the next generation do things so differently. For example as I watch parents of young children interact with their kids, my son and grandson included, I feel like I want to tell them what I think they are doing wrong. Now glory be to God, I have come to realize there are many ways to do things including raising children. Who said I was perfect in how I raised my children? They certainly can tell you how imperfect I was, but they and I know I did the best I could with what I had.

I believe each generation is a bit more evolved than the previous one, so if that is true, then they may know a better way to raise children. And my guess is some parents will do what I have done, look back and pass judgment on how they acted with their children. Instead, be gentle with yourself, you are always doing the best with what you have and know in every moment. Now it has taken me many, many years to learn this and allow it to be. I use to Monday-morning-quarterback my whole life and feel miserable at how I failed. Since I have come to understand and accept that I am always doing my best and committed to creating myself anew in the next grandest version of the greatest vision I ever held about myself, my life is so much easier and peaceful. This is thanks to Neale Donald Walsch and all his wonderful books which have been instrumental in my spiritual growth. I pray I have the honor of meeting Neale in person one day so I may thank him in person. Another wonderful realization is, we are all here to help one another, and in other words we are in service to all of life as life is in service to us.

Acknowledgements

I have so many to thank for my life and this book. First I want to thank you, the reader for taking a chance on my book. The magical three, my children; Christopher, Shelly and Brian for teaching me so much with your honesty, my daughter Shelly who literally saved me with her advocating on my behalf to keep me alive, and my doctors who have cared for me to this day, my amazing grandson, Darren who consistently reminds me how full of love we all are as he showers me with his love.

Whole Foods staff of Bellingham, Massachusetts for helping me during the first stroke; staff at Massachusetts General and Spaulding Rehab; Staff at Kindred healthcare in Dedham, MA; All my PCAs, all my friends, Kinsey, Bruce, Linda, Donna, Diane, Larissa just to name a few, My coach Max Ryan, My editor and friend Travis. Ron Hale, my publisher who graciously took on the publishing of my book. All of my clients and students who have believed in me and allowing me the honor of working with them some even after the stroke. God bless you all.

And of course my family of origin, my amazing parents and siblings, Richard, Bobby and Paula, who helped me grow into the person I am today. And never to forget all my spiritual mentors and teachers whom I have met only through their books and pray I get to meet in person to properly thank them for helping me be completely open to my spirituality and divine gifts. So much more to learn, experience and teach, glory be to God.

I must admit I am most grateful for my awareness, courage and faith in myself and all that is divine. I love myself and I love my life; thanks to **A Course in Miracles** and **Conversations with God** that helped me become aware that only love is real while all else is an illusion. This awareness has kept me going during the times that I may have wanted to give up. Let us remember to be grateful for ourselves and all we have.

Epilogue

Every day I wake up with huge gratitude in my heart for being alive and well, able to think, talk, exercise, meditate and pray, have my shake for breakfast then showered and ready for the day.

I have come to understand we are all perfectly imperfect as human beings. I believe it time for us to give up the struggle between ego and soul. I believe we all have a duality and battle going on inside us; ego vs. soul. Time to balance it all; mind, body and soul, at least in my most humble opinion for whatever it may be worth, for only you can decide for you.

We are in a very important time on earth. We are all, including planet earth, evolving into a higher dimension where material becomes less important as the realization that only love is real becomes more present in most lives. All my teachers have taught me about how we evolve and this concept of moving into the 5th dimension. It is not a place but a way of living. It is internal; it is where our truth lies as well as our happiness and heaven or hell. We only think what makes us happy or sad lives outside of us, but in truth, it is our thoughts that create our happiness or unhappiness. Oh I know, logic will dictate why we are happy or not, and that logic only exists in the 3rd dimension, in our mind. For in our soul, there is no logic, only pure peace, love, compassion, understanding, joy, fun and heaven.

Our mission, if we so choose, is to find the path to our souls. This was my mission after my second divorce. As a child I fully knew and was in my trusting place as most children are. We grow up with misunderstandings of truth so our souls can easily get covered up and thus our unhappiness and feeling of being in hell occur. In order to not feel hell, we try to cover it up with food, drugs, alcohol, entertainment, sex, tobacco, and alcohol, whatever it takes to feel better, as I did in the nursing home with food. But truth be told, I did not like myself fat, so I just chose to not think about it and continued to bury the bad feelings with food. I must admit, to this day, I still have a bit of struggle with it all, but I have discovered how to cope better so that I do not continue with any unhealthy habits. I am very fortunate to be a disciplined woman who loves structure while learning to be fully in the present moment with all the feelings that come and go at any given time.

I realize how blessed I am to be alive and independently living even though I may have days that I feel down, for being human can and will bring that on, it is what we choose to do when that happens that will set a tone in our reality. I chose to set intentions for my day, then go with the flow of life, drop the oars as Abraham would say, to go downstream on the river, that leads to our peace. What I have come to understand, this means letting go of control and expectations; set intentions, have faith and patience, keep your vibrations and energy clear and high and flow to your dreams being guided by your emotions.

I have a feeling my next book will be after I have found my partner, and on a speaking tour to inspire my audiences so you can see how Law of Attraction, Faith and Patience continue to work in my life. I will set my intentions and share with you my results.

I pray you feel blessed after reading this book and please accept my gratitude for your patience and time. Sending you much love until I have the good fortune and honor of meeting you!

MANY BLESSINGS, LOVE AND NAMASTE,
Joanne M. Susi

CF
at
Pri
FFC

'lA information can be obtained
ww.ICGtesting.com
'ed in the USA
W05n0512140116